The Extravagant Gift

Every Person's Path to Salvation

Jerry Schemmel

To _____

From _____

Message:

In an awesome and majestic display
of power and purpose, God created the world.

The Bible tells of one holy, supreme and perfect
God creating the earth out of his great love.

In the beginning,
God created the heavens and the earth.
Genesis 1:1

And then God, in his unmatched wisdom and love, created the first human being.

God's other creations were "made." But Adam was "formed" by God from the dirt of the earth, thus showing a great accuracy, exactness and specialness - unlike any living thing on earth.

When the Lord made the earth and the heavens...
the Lord formed man from the dust of the ground
and breathed into his nostrils the breath of life, and
man became a living being.
Genesis 2:4-7

God then decided to create the first woman, who
would be named Eve.

God made the first woman not from dust, but from
man's flesh and bone.

In so doing, he showed us that in marriage, which
Adam and Eve entered into, man and woman
symbolically become one flesh.

*But for Adam no suitable helper was found. So the
Lord God caused the man to fall into a deep sleep;
and while he was sleeping, he took one of the man's
ribs and closed up the place with flesh. Then the
Lord God made a woman from the rib he had taken
out of the man, and brought her to the man.
The man said,
"This is now bone of my bones and flesh of my
flesh; she shall be called 'woman,'
for she was taken out of man."
For this reason a man will leave his father and
mother and be united to his wife, and they will
become one flesh.*
Genesis 2:20-24

Because of his great love for the people he created, God gave them a free will. He granted Adam and Eve the ability to think on their own, to make their own decisions.

God told Adam that he was free to eat from any tree in the Garden of Eden, except for one.

God did not physically prevent Adam from eating the fruit from this tree. He simply gave Adam a choice, thus the possibility of choosing wrongly.

The Lord God took the man and put him in the Garden of Eden to work it and take care of it. And the Lord God commanded the man, "You are free to eat from any tree in the garden; but you must not eat from the tree of the knowledge of good and evil, for when you eat it you will surely die.
Genesis 2:15-17

But both Adam and Eve disobeyed God's
commands. They ate the forbidden fruit.

Like all of us have done at times in our lives,
Adam and Eve disobeyed God.
They chose wrong instead of right.

*When the woman saw that the fruit of the tree was
good for food and pleasing to the eye, and also
desirable for gaining wisdom, she took some and
ate it. She also gave some to her husband,
who was with her, and he ate it.*
Genesis 3:6

Because they disobeyed God, Adam and Eve would
suffer the consequences of their actions,
just as God had warned them.

They were punished and cast into a life separated
from God.

To the woman, God said, "I will greatly increase your pains in childbearing; with pain you will give birth to children. Your desire will be for your husband and he will rule over you.
To Adam he said, "Because you listened to your wife and ate from the tree about which I commanded you, 'You must not eat of it,' "Cursed is the ground because of you; through painful toil you will eat of it all the days of your life. It will produce thorns and thistles for you, and you will eat the plants of the field."
Genesis 3:16-18

Everyone has disobeyed God.

It started with Adam and Eve
and continues with us today.

All of us have strayed away like sheep.
We have left God's path to follow our own.
Romans 6:23

We are all aware of God's commands for our lives.

We know right from wrong, good from evil.

Yet, for various reasons,
all of us make wrong choices.

*If we claim to be without sin, we deceive ourselves
and the truth is not in us.*
1 John 1:8

We sin.

Sometimes we are very subtle with our sins and
sometimes we are quite blatant.

But we all stray from God.

*For all have sinned and fall short
of the glory of God.*
Romans 3:23

As he did with the first sinners, Adam and Eve,
God tells us that breaking his commands, that
sinning, has consequences.

God declares that those who sin will be cut off from
him and be sent to an existence without him.

The punishment for sin, God says, is death. Not an
instant death of one's body, but a spiritual death in
the form of a separation from him.

For the wages of sin is death.
Romans 6:23

But there is great news!

In fact, it is the greatest news mankind
has ever known!

Despite our wrongdoing, God wants us. He loves us
with a love that is so deep we can hardly fathom it.
His desire is to forgive our sins
and bring us back to him.

God has given us the means to overcome
sin and its consequences.

He has given us the chance to be saved
from our sins.

This is my commitment to my people:
removal of their sins.
Romans 11:27

God's promise to us is that our sins will be
completely erased.

And completely forgotten.

He will not simply forgive. He will forget.

For I will forgive their wickedness and remember their sins no more.
Hebrews 8:12

As the means to forgiveness of sins and a reunion with God, he has given us his son, Jesus Christ.

They shall call his name Immanuel,
which means "God With Us."
Mathew 1:23

Moved by a passion for his human creation,
God became one.

The bible equates Jesus with God,
that they were one.

He was, at once, God and man.

In Christ there is all of God in a human body.
Colossians 2:9

To show his extravagant love for his children, he walked the earth among us. He felt our pain, endured our sorrows.

God, by being one with his son, Jesus Christ, walked in our shoes.

Why would God endure earth's pain? So we would know that he knows how we feel.

That's how much he loves us.

He was tempted in every way that we are,
but he did not sin.
Hebrews 4:15

God the father, sent Jesus the son, into to the world
to save us from our sins.

He didn't give us rules or guidelines or mandates.

Motivated by love, he gave himself.

The son of man did not come to be served, but to serve, and give his life as a ransom for many.
Mathew 20:28

Even though he never committed a sin,
Jesus was condemned to death.

He was crucified and suffered an excruciatingly
painful death.

But his death was for a reason –
it was the payment for our sins.

*He canceled the record that contained the charges
against us. He destroyed it by nailing it
to Christ's cross.*
Colossians 2:14

God loves us so much that he allowed Jesus, his
own son, to pay our debt,
to serve our sentence.

*God made him who had no sin to be sin for us, so
that in him we may become
the righteousness of God.*
2 Corinthians 5:21

Our sins have been placed not on us, but on Jesus.
Christ has taken the blow for us.
He has served our sentence.

Jesus took our sin upon himself and invited
God to punish it.

This is God's free gift to us.

It is called GRACE.

Christ was offered once to bear the sins of many.
Hebrews 9:28

Receiving this free gift of grace from
God is incredibly easy.

We must simply believe in Jesus.

...everyone who looks to the Son and believes in him shall have eternal life...
John 6:40

All that is required to have your sins forgiven and
your spot secured in heaven is to believe in
God's son.

Nothing more.

And nothing less.

Those who believe in the son have eternal life.
John 3:36

This is how Christianity differs from all other religions.

All other religions are based, to some extent, on works. Works is the idea that one must work his way into God's favor - that one must *do* something for God so that God will *do* something for him. Works says you must earn your way to God.

But Christianity says salvation is not through works.

It is only through faith in Christ.

I am the way, the truth and the life. No one comes to the father but through me.
John 14:6

The bible says there is never enough you can do for
God to earn his approval.

God's standard is perfection. And we will never,
ever be perfect.

That's why God gave us his son.

I am the light of the world. Whoever follows me will never walk in darkness, but will have the light of life.
John 8:12

God has declared that salvation is through grace.

And nothing else.

Works are not required – just faith.

God's love does not depend on what we do for him.

For it is by grace that you have been saved, through faith – and this is not from yourselves, it is the gift of God – not by works, so that no one can boast.
Ephesians 2:8-9

Please know that Jesus, your personal savior,
wants you.

He wants to be in your life,
no matter what you've done.

He doesn't care about where you've been.
He only cares about where you're going.

Jesus longs for you.

He is waiting. He is searching the horizon for a
glimpse of his lost child.

He is looking for you.

...neither death nor life, neither angels nor demons, neither the present nor the future, nor any powers, neither height nor depth, nor anything else in all creation, will be able to separate us from the love of God that is in Christ Jesus our Lord.
Romans 8:38, 39

God is extending a personal invitation to have your sins forgiven and your spot in heaven secured through Jesus.

Behold, I stand at the door and knock: if any one
hears my voice, and opens the door,
I will come in to him.
Revelation 3:20

The invitation is simple and clear. God is precise in what he asks for and precise in what he gives.

There are no requirements, no strings attached. No baptism needed. No church attendance required. No lifestyle changes mandated. No repetitive prayers. No pilgrimage to Mecca.

It's very simple: Belief for salvation.

For God so loved the world that he gave his one and only son, that whoever believes in him shall not perish but have everlasting life.
John 3:16

If you accept Jesus Christ as your savior,
he will give you everlasting life.

And he will give you so much more.

He will change you.

A word of warning if you let him take up
residence in your heart:

You'll never be the same again.

Therefore, if anyone is in Christ, he is new creation;
the old has gone, the new has come.
2 Corinthians 5:17

Jesus will give you everything to live for.

*If anyone believes in me, rivers of living water will
flow out from that person's heart.*
John 7:38

And he will give you everything to die for.

*I am the resurrection and the life. He who believes
in me will live, even though he dies.*
John 11:25

We have two choices.

We can reject Jesus. Or we can accept him.

What should I do with Jesus,
the one called the Christ?
Mathew 27:21

Rejecting Jesus is clearly an option.
Many have taken it.

We can decide that this idea of Jesus being God's
son and our personal savior is just too far-fetched,
too fantastic to be true.

We can conclude that we are too wary,
that the decision is too risky.

*He was despised and rejected by men, a man of
sorrows, and familiar with suffering.*
Isaiah 53:3

Or, we can accept him.

Option two is to believe in him, follow him, embrace him and have him live in us forever.

We can refuse to walk away from this offer. We can take the hand of Jesus and let him lead us to his father. To our father.

This is how God showed his love among us. He sent his one and only son into the world that we might live through him.
1 John 4:9

One of God's great gifts is the gift of choice. He gave it to Adam and Eve and he gives to us.

He allows us to decide for ourselves about his son. God will never insist. He won't even interfere.

It's completely your decision: Reject or accept.

God has come to your house, has stepped to your door and knocked. It is completely up to you whether or not you let him in.

Behold, I stand at the door, and knock: if anyone
hears my voice, and opens the door,
I will come in to him.
Revelation 3:20

If you wish to accept God's free gift of grace,
you can do it now.

If you wish to have all your sins forgiven and your
spot in heaven secured, it can be done right now.

All you who are thirsty, come and drink.
Isaiah 55:1

There are no magic words, no specific language.

It is not about content. It's about a decision - a decision to accept Jesus Christ as your Lord and Savior. It's about a decision to simply believe.

God's grace:

You can't earn it.
You don't deserve it.
All you can do is accept it.

For God so loved the world that he gave his only son, that whoever believes in him will never die, but have eternal life.
John 3:16

If you want to make that decision, right now,
just pray a simple prayer.

Please turn to the next page –

and turn to your savior.

GOD WANTS TO GIVE YOU AN
EXTRAVAGENT GIFT!

Dear God, I know that I am a sinner. And I know
I can't save myself from my sins. I want my sins
washed away by the blood of Christ.
This very moment, Lord, I want to accept your son,
Jesus Christ, as my savior.

I believe that he was your son, God, that he died on
a cross as punishment for my sins,
that he served my sentence for me.
God, I want to open up my heart, right now,
and let Jesus live there.
I want my sins forgiven
and my spot in heaven secured.
I want to be saved.
I want Jesus Christ.
Amen.

*I tell you, there is rejoicing in the presence of the
angels of God over one sinner who repents.*
Luke 15:10

CPSIA information can be obtained
at www.ICGtesting.com
Printed in the USA
FSOW01n2304030516
20011FS

9 781606 471548